Neighborhood Safari

Rabbits

by Dalton Rains

FOCUS READERS®
PIONEER

www.focusreaders.com

Focus Readers is distributed by North Star Editions:
sales@northstareditions.com | 888-417-0195

Produced for Focus Readers by Red Line Editorial.

Photographs ©: Shutterstock Images, cover, 1, 4, 6, 8, 10, 12, 14, 17, 18, 21

Library of Congress Cataloging-in-Publication Data
Names: Rains, Dalton, author.
Title: Rabbits / by Dalton Rains.
Description: Mendota Heights, MN: Focus Readers, [2025] | Series: Neighborhood safari | Includes bibliographical references and index. | Audience: Grades K-1
Identifiers: LCCN 2023059793 (print) | LCCN 2023059794 (ebook) | ISBN 9798889981787 (hardcover) | ISBN 9798889982340 (paperback) | ISBN 9798889983453 (pdf) | ISBN 9798889982906 (ebook)
Subjects: LCSH: Rabbits--Juvenile literature | Rabbits--Anatomy--Juvenile literature | Rabbits--Behavior--Juvenile literature | Rabbits--Life cycles--Juvenile literature
Classification: LCC QL737.L32 R35 2025 (print) | LCC QL737.L32 (ebook) | DDC 599.32--dc23/eng/20240123
LC record available at https://lccn.loc.gov/2023059793
LC ebook record available at https://lccn.loc.gov/2023059794

Printed in the United States of America
Mankato, MN
082024

About the Author

Dalton Rains is a writer and editor from Minnesota.

Table of Contents

Chapter 1

Running Rabbits

A rabbit nibbles on grass. Then, it hears a twig snap. The rabbit freezes. It sees a fox creeping closer. The rabbit runs away. It is safe from the **predator**.

Rabbits often live in areas near trees and bushes. Most live in **burrows**. These are holes rabbits dig in the ground. Some kinds of rabbits live with others. They make groups of burrows. These are called warrens.

Fun Fact

Not all rabbits live in burrows. Some live in nests above the ground.

Chapter 2

Body Parts

Rabbits are **mammals**. They have soft fur all over their bodies. They also have short, fluffy tails. Rabbits have strong hind legs.

ear
eye
fur
tooth
leg

A rabbit has two long ears on top of its head. It has two eyes. A rabbit also has 28 teeth. Six of the teeth are sharp. They can cut through grass. The rest of the teeth are used for chewing.

Fun Fact

Rabbits come in different colors. Their fur may be brown, gray, black, or white.

Chapter 3

Hopping and Hearing

Rabbits are fast. Their strong hind legs help them run quickly. Rabbits use their front legs to dig burrows. They can hide in these burrows. Rabbits' fur color also helps them hide.

Rabbits use their large ears to hear predators. They can twist their ears almost all the way around. They can hear sounds from more than 1 mile (1.6 km) away. The ears also help heat and cool rabbits.

At night, rabbits make a special kind of poop. They eat it to get more **nutrients**.

Lots of Babies

Rabbits can have babies at a young age. And female rabbits are **pregnant** for only one month. They give birth to four or five **litters** each year. A litter may have up to seven babies.

Chapter 4

A Rabbit's Life

Baby rabbits are called kittens or kits. Kits are born **blind**. Their eyes open after about 10 days. A week later, they explore outside the burrow.

At first, the kits' mother **nurses** them. When kits are three weeks old, they stop drinking their mother's milk. One to two weeks later, they leave the burrow for good. Most rabbits **mate** when they are four or five months old.

Fun Fact

Most wild rabbits live for a year or less. Some may live for three years or more.

Life Cycle

Kits are born blind.
Kits' eyes open after about 10 days.
A week after opening their eyes, kits explore outside their burrows.
Kits move out of their burrows after four to five weeks.
Most rabbits can mate and have their own babies after 12 weeks.

FOCUS ON

Rabbits

Write your answers on a separate piece of paper.

1. Write a sentence describing how rabbits use their legs.
2. Would you want a rabbit to live near your home? Why or why not?
3. For how long are female rabbits pregnant?
   A. about one week
   B. about one month
   C. about one year
4. Why might rabbits live in burrows?
   A. to get closer to predators
   B. to find food that is buried
   C. to hide from predators

Answer key on page 24.

Glossary

blind
Unable to see.

burrows
Holes or tunnels that an animal digs to use as its home.

litters
Groups of babies born to a mother at one time.

mammals
Animals that have hair and feed their babies milk.

mate
To come together to make a baby.

nurses
Feeds a baby milk from the mother's body.

nutrients
Things that people, animals, and plants need to stay healthy.

predator
An animal that hunts other animals for food.

pregnant
Growing a baby.

To Learn More

BOOKS

An, Priscilla. *Rabbit Behavior.* Minneapolis: Abdo Publishing, 2023.

Gaertner, Meg. *Life Cycle of a Rabbit.* Mendota Heights, MN: Focus Readers, 2022.

NOTE TO EDUCATORS

Visit **www.focusreaders.com** to find lesson plans, activities, links, and other resources related to this title.

Index

Answer Key: 1. Answers will vary; **2.** Answers will vary; **3.** B; **4.** C